Janny Bowman was born in Elgin, brought up in Lossiemouth and now lives in Dundee. Married at 17, a week before she turned 18, she and her husband, Godon, have been through more downs than ups, their strength and determination keeping them together. They have 3 children and 6 grandchildren and live with 5 dachshunds. Many of her poems are her life experiences.

I dedicate this book to my family who have lifted me up when I have been down, they have given me the inspiration to write about them.

Janny Bowman

A LIFE OF REFLECTIONS

AUSTIN MACAULEY PUBLISHERS®

LONDON ∗ CAMBRIDGE ∗ NEW YORK ∗ SHARJAH

A CIP catalogue record for this title is available from the British Library.

ISBN 9781035834648 (Paperback)
ISBN 9781035834655 (ePub e-book)

www.austinmacauley.com

First Published 2025
Austin Macauley Publishers Ltd®
1 Canada Square
Canary Wharf
London
E14 5AA

I would like to thank Gill Hunt and Steve Flynn for their help in getting my poems to be sent to my publisher.

Table of Contents

The Man from Inverness

There was a man
From Inverness
He was full of plooks
His face was a mess

He went to the shop
Bought haggis, tattie and neep
I'll have it for ma tea he said
Before I go to sleep

He went to the library
And books he did carry
On the way home
He met his friend Harry

Harry lived beside him
He was married to Beryl his wife
She had a big bottom
It had been big all her life

Bob got home to
Have his tea
Of haggis, neeps
And mashed tattie

He read his book
In a cosy nook
It mentioned a man
Who couldn't cook

The nights drew in
And his wife came in
She was carrying a bag
Of cakes for her sins

They had the cakes
With a cup of tea
Then they went to bed
Night-night they both said

The Monster

It was a chilly December night
And Jamie went to bed
Thinking about monsters
That lurked about in his head

The monster it was blue
And it slept behind the door
It didn't have a blanket
As it lay on the floor

The monster he had
Eyes of sky blue
And the warts he had
There was a good few

He was big he was fat
Was all lumpy and bumpy
He was roundish in shape
Like "Humpty Dumpty"

Because of chocolate
The monster was real
It looked like it had been
Run over by a wheel

He was big he was ugly
And in his mind he would start
To stand and let off
A muckle big fart

Jamie was tired
And went to sleep
And the monster it went
Back into his mind so deep

For it didn't exist
But to Jamie it did
As he went to bed
With a monster called "Sid"!

The Royal Mail

The Royal Mail
There is nothing better
Than waiting on
A parcel, card or letter

A parcel you ordered
Or a surprise you've been sent
From people in your life
Who have come and went

Birthday and Xmas cards
A check with money
A bill you have to pay
That makes you worry

Into the post office
Standing in a queue
Sore legs standing
I wish I could take a pew

It's my turn next
To get my stamps
Buy gas and electric
Pay this and that

I get home and my
Post is on the floor
It's junk mail rubbish
who could ask for more!

Who knows what
Tomorrow will bring
Maybe there will be something
That will make me sing…

A card, a letter or appointment
I have been waiting for
Or will it be a reminder
That will land at my door?

The Summer Holiday

We went a summer holiday
To Great Yarmouth one year
We stayed in a caravan
Not that far from the peer

It was our summer holiday
We were to stay in a caravan
Me, Gordon and the dogs
Not forgetting Aunty Anne!

The weather was amazing
The sun was shining bright
The dogs were out basking
Then two of them decided to fight!

I broke it up and gave them a row
The woman next door was wondering how
"Did you nae hear them barking?" I quickly said
She gave a look and shook her head!

Tom Brown

Tom went to the doctor's
With a headache one day
It lasted all night
And then into the next day

He headed for home
Got in and sat down
Upon his face
He had a frown

The pain got worse
And his head did burst
Had a bleed in his brain
And then the angel came

She took him to heaven
He was 77
His grave stone the following read
If your reading this
I Tom Brown am truly dead!

Winning Money!

Winning money....
Would it make me happy?
I always dream
Of winning the lottery

The weight of worry
Would be lifted
From heavy shoulders
But who would be gifted?

I wouldn't be greedy,
Conceited or snotty
But winning the lottery
Would make me dotty

But destined to do without
Is the reality that shouts!
And so I take my dreams to bed
And count my money I could spend!

Wishes

A penny for your wishes
Asks the wishing well
Will they be in heaven?
Or will someone wish for hell

I could wish for so much
But I wish for one thing
Simple and not haunting
But thinking of it, it is too daunting!

Words

A bird flies in the wind so high
With their beautiful wings
Magpies and starlings and
The mockingbird who sings

They fly dead slow
When they hover above
With the wind beneath them
Some land on a glove

The Hawk will land
To get some dinner
So when he catches a mouse
He knows he's the winner

It would be a wonderful thing
If we could fly
Fly to places
High up in the sky

The feeling of not
Being heavy but light
Soaring free
What a wonderful sight.

Roast Pork

Roast pork with apple sauce
I love this and all because
It is my favourite roast dinner
They go so well it is a winner

Served with carrots and roast potatoes
Gravy and some crackling
It is a meal to look forward to
Like bacon and eggs or a nice beef stew

For food I love
Savoury or sweet
In all its forms
It goes down a treat

But my favourite has to be roast pork
Sweet and sour or just a roast
Roast pork and apple
Are like tea and toast!

The Crisp

I come in a packet
All colourful and bright
My packet is square
For this wonderful delight

Many flavours I can be
Plain, cheesy or vinegary
Tomato, beef and pickled onion
To name but a few I've missed out summin

Round, square
Wiggly and hollow
Whatever your kind
I'm a crunch and a swallow

Crunchy, tangy and tasty
Your taste buds are going
The saliva in your mouth
Well, it just starts a flowing

I'm a wonderful snack
Can be eaten any time of day
Morning noon and night
Whatever comes what may

Tunnocks Biscuits

Soft and creamy
And oh so dreamy
Is the centre of the cake
Crumbly wafers and chewy centres
Are some of their wonderful bakes

Covered in chocolate
Dark or milk
The texture of the chocolate
Feels like silk

Chewy, creamy
And served with a cuppy
Coffee or tea
Whatever you fancy

You open the wrapper
And to your delight
A caramel wafer
A wondrous sight.

Ward Food

A cup of tea or coffee
And a digestive to go with it
"just milk in mine, no sugar
And yes I'll have a biscuit"

A jug of water with some ice
To keep us from dehydrating
At 1 o'clock it's dinnertime
For our food we're anticipating

Soup and a sandwich and also pudding
It really was quite nice
With tea and biscuits at 3 o'clock
This should really quite suffice!

Little Time

There is no pill
For a broken heart
But I guess I knew
That from the start

There is only time
For the pain to heal
So I must wait
For me to heal

The "nutter" ward I've landed in
Like all the rest I've committed a sin
But my crime was life
And what it dealt
My mind couldn't cope
with the cards I'd been dealt

The never-ending tragedies
One after another
Out with my powers
And so I must suffer

Time the great healer
The answer to all
Time will lift me up
As I continue to fall
Into the depths of despair

This frightening place
But in time I will heal
And have a smile on my face

Black Days

Black days my mind a haze
What am I to do?
Despair and no laughter
Is how it feels for ever after?

The pain I'm in
Is a terrible sin
The torment is torture
I cannot win

For the feeling of nothing
Of numbness as if dead
With all of the shit
That goes on in my head!

Oh help me God
For guidance and salvation
For I feel as if I have death
By invitation

For it beckons me
To come and see
If it will be the
Death of me!

So with some help
Starts the healing
And death to me
Is no longer appealing

For I can see that
We all have a choice
As we listen inside
To the infamous voice!

My Mental Health

My mental health
My life is grim
The lights go out
Everything goes dim

Dim and black
In the deepest hole
It's taken over my life
It's taken out my soul!

I feel all a loss
Agitated and sad
I hear that damn voices
They drive me mad

They tell me I'm ugly
Fat and obtuse
That I'm good for nothing
And really no use!

I put on a face
For others to see
Easier that way
Well, it's easier for me…

New Year and More Worries

Another poem
Of what's gone on
My list of worries
Goes on and on

Thinking of the past
And all that has happened
Leaves me nothing less
Than saddened

So to New Year I say this
Be good to me this year
And...
Don't take the piss

Don't laden me with worry
Upset and strife
I am wanting
To love my life

To be at peace
With my oneself
With all of the people who touch my life
From me to you, your loving wife....

More Tears

New Year more tears
Was what happened then
With arguing and alcohol
And fighting after ten….

Infused by drink
It caused a stink
And for what broke loose
Fighting and all inside my house

The outcome was rather bleak
My hubby couldn't take it
Driven to the edge
Between us lies a wedge

For his life he did try and take
With some sleeping pills
He went to bed wishing he was dead
Coz of too much shit running through his head

Thankfully I was alerted
As to what he had done
And phoned 999
For an ambulance to come!

He is ok
was caught in time
From ending his life
And not being mine

We live with the consequences
Of what he has done
The guilt and disbelief
Is second to none

And so my soulmate for over 30 years
Has got to heal and mend
As his mind and the event
Drives him round the bend

So a Happy New Year
That it was not
The truth is out
Some people can rot!

Sorrow

With a heavy heart
And another sigh
The tears they come
And so I cry

But tears are good
To help get the pain out
But I want to scream
And I want to shout

Tears are good
They help me to heal
Heal the pain
I continue to feel

They help get rid
of a darkened day
So they keep telling me
So they say!

Worries

Another poem
Of what's gone on
My list of worries
Goes on and on

Thinking of the past
And all that has happened
Leaves me nothing less
Than saddened

So to "New Year" I say this
Be good to me
This year
And don't take the piss

Don't laden me with worry
Upset and strife
I want to be able
To love my life

To be at peace with
One and all
|I leave it up to you
It is your call

At the Gym

At the gym twice a week
We listen to music and Anna speak
"Come on girls get to the beat,
Lift your arms your legs and feet"

Sweat starts forming on my head
Oh how I wish I was still in bed!
Stretching limbs back and fore
Moving my bits like never before!

I need a drink I'm awfully dry
I gulp it down with a heavy sigh
Gearing myself up for another session
If only with food I had learned my lesson

"Right then girls how we doing?"
Personally I'm about spewing
We'll do some ball work for a bit
I'm lying on the floor, thinking, "Oh shit"!

Right we are done it's just my weight
How much I have lost I anticipate
I stand in ore looking in dismay
Of what the blasted scales did say

"Well, you have lost 2 pounds this week, that's good"
When all I think about is food

Food and its cooking and not to fry it
"Oh help me god while I'm on my diet!"

Car Crashes

You see what's coming
It's in slow motion
Everything just stops
As your heart it nearly stops

Lucky to survive
Which could have been
Disaster
For now and forever after

One of these accidents
That I had
Wrote off the car
And I was sad

For a Volvo I had been driving
Went off the road and into the trees
I spun in the air saying
"Help me please"

And all I could see
Were the trees
Which I thought
They're going to be the death of me

Well, I spun up in the air
Facing the trees I was in despair
But luck for me I landed
Between 2 trees

I was concussed
But didn't know
As I tried to walk home
It was going too slow

Petrified of being in the dark
Not knowing where I was
I felt so ill and sick with worry
I needed home but couldn't hurry

Well, a man did stop
And asked if I was ok
He took me home
I showed him the way

Home I got sick with worry
Telling Gordy what had happened
Of my accident in the Volvo
This had left him deeply saddened

The Volvo was his car
Which I had written off
And the angel on my shoulder
Well, she nearly fell off!

Caught in the Middle

Caught in the middle of a furious fight
Caught in the middle just didn't seem right
In the wrath of anger, spit and pain
Life would never be the same….

Because of one persons
Lack of respect
The wise words that were spoken
Had little or no effect

A total lack of adoration
And looking up to a generation
Meant they were right and we were wrong
And so the fight well it just went on

And so it shall continue
The photograph's memory
Will remain in situ
Waiting for answers only time can tell
Until then…I'd be as well in hell!

Changed Days

When I was young
And rather wee
It's all different now
As far as I can see!

From red phone boxes
That needed 2p's
That were small
And smelled of pee

Rounders, Kirby
And going to the park
We had to play out
From morning to dark!

Now there are "I" pads
Mobile phones and computers
That pass the day
In a technical stupor!

Twin tubs
To automatics
And then the microwave
You had no mod cons
You were just a kitchen slave

TVs were round
And rather fat
You didn't have
Sky, Virgin or that

Now they are bigger
And rather thin
The slimmer the better
You just can't win

Betamax video and tape recorders
All of them in different orders
Now it's "I" pads
Netflix, YouTube and such
Thinking of it all, it's a bit too much

Singing

When I was young
And in my prime
I started to sing
I think I was nine

My knuckles would get wrapped
With a knitting needle
From a nun in Elgin
She was a horrid weasel

I moved from there
And went to a different lady
She said that I
Could "sing like a Linty"

I sung in the school choir
I sung in the town hall
I won a singing contest
I was having a ball!

I still go back to when I was young
Singing Neil Reids "Mother of mine"
But now as an adult, I get all outta puff
My voice is husky and a bit rough!

I enjoy the Karaoke
I think I am no other
I sing along to anything
I used to sing to my mother

Singing makes me happy
As you all well can see
From singing "La la la to"
"Tra-ra-ra-llee!"

Embarrassing Moment!

I was going out one night
But glanced down to my feet
No nails to paint…
So false ones were a treat!

I had attentively glued them on
With some super glue
I thought that's done the trick
And stuck them in my shoes

So off out with Gordy
To a wedding dance
I could see his boss was there
I see him at a glance

Well, his boss came over
Looking for a dance
My feet looked fine
And so I started to prance…

But all the time I was thinking
About my glued on nails
Hoping they would stay on
And the glue wouldn't fail…

Dancing away thinking I was cool
I looked down at my feet
And boy did I feel a fool
Well, one nail was off
What was I to do?
Coz my nails weren't hidden

In this type of shoe…
The music did stop
And off I did trot
With my nail from the floor
I headed towards the toilet door

So in the end with nothing I could do
I stuck my foot back in my shoe
For vanity had embarrassed me, dear
In having no nails was my biggest fear!

"Emotions"

Sometimes I'm happy
Sometimes I'm sad
Sometimes I'm good
And sometimes I'm bad!

Feeling happy and full of glee
The sight of a Xmas tree
The decorations and all of that "tat"
Makes me giggle at this and that

From dancing snowmen
And carol singing
It is a time
For loving and giving

A time to reflect on
Xmas past
Was it as good as the last?
A time for peace in your heart and soul
To wish for something better, that's your goal

I feel sad and angry
At the years gone by
At all the shit
I ask myself why?

The cards I've been dealt
I have no control over
I wish I could find me
A four-leaf clover!

Fibromyalgia

Fibromyalgia
The dreaded curse
When you dinna cane
Fit pain is worst

Be it from your neck
Down to your toes
How it starts
Nobody knows

The pain is horrific
Muscle spasms and tingling
This becomes even worse
When you have it all mingling

Chronic pain
And chronic fatigue
Makes this illness
In its own league.

Forgetting

I keep forgetting everything
It's taking over my life
It used to be a slow thing
So now it seems quite rife

My memory is not as good
As it was a few years back
And so my mind is a jumble
Of organisation which I lack

Trying to remember
The messages and such
Trying to remember
It's all become too much!

Phone numbers and conversations
Of what has just been said
It's like my memory has gone
I feel sometimes is dead!

Appointments on the calendar
Or a message on the phone
I've forgotten what it all entailed
Because my memory has gone

So to sum this up I was going to say
But somehow I can't remember

Coz my memory has left the building
Let's hope it's not forever!

Going Home

I'm going back home
I'm sitting on the bus
I'm going this way
Coz it's a lot less fuss

I'm up on a visit
Excited as I am
To see my two sisters
And of course my mum…

To see my mum
And give her a bosey
To wrap my arms round her
And make her all cosy

To see her excites me
And brings on a smile
For I haven't seen her
It's been quite a while

I write these words
In my mind I hoard
I write them down
Because I am bored

To pass the time
The hour and the day
I write them down
In my own special way

Telling a story
And rhyming the word
Putting pen to paper
Sometimes it's absurd….

Growing Older

Growing older and the years roll in
I have to accept my double chin
My grey hair and my wrinkles too
And those funny spots to name but a few

From creaking bones
And joints that stick
The pain and the agony
Makes you sick

My growing waist line and funny bumps
That just appears in funny old lumps
The once straight back now has a stoop
I wish all this would go and poop!

It's never-ending; there will be false teeth
To grace their presence at my disbelief
A pair of gnashers in a jar
Reminding me of memories from afar

So all of this
I sit and embrace as
I sit back and look
At my wrinkled face!

Growing older you should have more sense
To think about what you do
The choices you make
The decisions you've made
Paths chosen but a few

I Often Wonder

I often wonder
Where I went wrong
And now…
There are no words to my song

I often wonder
Where I would be
Without you
Beside me

I often think back
To when we were young
When we were good
And life was fun

But growing old
Has not been so good
Life and its problems
I don't mean to sound rude

What can we do?
To carry on
And find words
To sing a different song

To be together
United and content

What hurt I've caused you
Was never meant

It's Time to Go

It's time to go and rest your head
Upon the angel's wings
It's time to go dear sweetheart
Where the mockingbird always sings

It's time to go and say goodbye
To those you've left behind
It's time to go to the "Gates of Heaven"
Up above all of mankind

It's time to go
Where the stars shine bright
Where all is dark
In the middle of the night

In the day up above the clouds so far
By our side forever you are
So long be at peace and enjoy your rest
Because to us Mam you were simply the best…

In loving memory of my dear mam
Margaret Mitchell Jackson
Who sadly passed away
On 9 September 2015 aged 74 years

Mixed Emotions

And holding back the tears
You'd think I'd be used to it
After all these years

The pain of separation
And leaving behind
Family and friends
That is on my mind

The fun and the laughter
The cups of tea
Sitting round the table
Will stay close to me

So I say my goodbyes
With a heavy heart
Memories coming home with me
For when I go home again
We'll just have to wait and see…

Our Kaleb

Blonde hair and blue eyes
And a really infectious grin
Who loves going out
With his mam and dad for a swim

He loves to swim
Like a water baby
He could one day
Be in the Olympics maybe

He likes going down a slide
It can't be fast enough
He loves to play with his mam and dad
He likes a bit of rough

He loves his food
He's like a gull
His belly's never empty
It's always full

He loves to bury
In his mam's bosey
Where he feels safe
Warm and cosy

He dotes on his dad
They have an incurable bond
He shakes with excitement
As he puts out his hand

He loves his blanket
His sooky cover
Blue and stinky
There is no other

Outside he loves
The feel of a worm
As he holds it in his hand
And makes it squirm!

So this is our Kaleb
My munchkin my soldier
He's all of this now
I can't wait till he's older!

London

London Bridge is falling down
Who is he who has a frown?
Is he a man or is he a ghost?
In London he is a host

Big Ben standing tall and bright
In the middle of the night
With the tower of London standing tall
And the houses of parliament looking so small

The River Thames runs all the way through
Housing boats, barges and bridges
Running for miles keeping London going
But who is he who's always moaning?

So as he stands there focused and canny
Who is this a ghost or a manny?
Standing there in the dead of night
Ready to give you a fright!

Lossiemouth

Up to Lossie
What will I see
Coz my face is a picture
Coz I'm full of glee

For the East
and the West beaches are two
Of the beautiful sights
To name but a few

The East beach with crashing waves
And an esplanade on shore
Then you have Miele's for ice-cream
Or Rizzas next door

The harbour and marina are next
What a beautiful picture
Pity that the flats
Are a permanent fixture

Walking your way round the town
Quaint houses you will see
In this picturesque toon
Loved especially by me!

So walking around by the harbour
Passing pubs on the run
You'll come to the golf course
If you fancy a "hole in one"

To the West beach that is next
With the lighthouse in view
And "Silver Sands"
In permanent situ

Passing the "posh" houses
When you come off the beach
In a price range I'm afraid
Is way out of my reach!

Then round to the camp
And R.A.F. base
This is my hometown
And I think it's just ace!

My First Job

My first job!
Well, what can I say?
I stood and shelled
Stinky prawns all day!

There was a knack I breaking their back
Getting them out whole
You had to get the tail out
This was your goal!

But shelling wasn't the job for me
Too slow I was in the company
So put onto the "blower" to blow the buggers out
I stood at the machine and washed them out!

This lasted for a while
But my quota wasn't up
So in desperation they said
We'll move you up to the top shed

Now the top shed was the place to be
There was Liz, Debbie and me
Many memories I have with me
Of the happy times that were good
Working for a living at "Seagull Seafood's"

On the Bus

On the bus sitting here
Squashed in, children near
Crumpled tickets on the floor
Talk and blether, noise galore!

The bell beeps for the bus to stop
And folks get off with a skip and a hop
Next person on, comes in with a pram
And to try and get off, it's like a traffic jam

Beeper again to the next destination
And the next person stands in anticipation
Passing traffic, houses and shops
All this I see and then it's my stop

This joggilee bus
The jingle of money
Please let me off
Coz this isn't funny!

On the Road

Passing time
My headphones are on
Flicking through my I pod
Searching for a song

Looking at signs
And trees in the fields
The sheep and crops
Make farmers yields

The houses the tractors
Land Rovers to boot
Caravans, sheds
And outbuildings to suit

Passing the time
I listen to drivel
Listening to songs
Skipping the middle

I've only got an hour to go
To amuse myself
God!
This road is so slow

So I'll eat up my sandwich
For my dinner
Cheese and ham
Is sure a winner

So to finish this off
This drivel of shite
I've told you this story
With all my might

Out in the Country

Out in the country
In the morning sun
In a big open space
And being at peace with one!

The birdies are tweeting
And singing their songs
Ants building their nests
And old men in string vests

Walking in the clean fresh air
I stand on a cow pat
And feel the despair!

Berries in the bushes
And bluebells in the grass
There is lots to see in the country
When you're out and when you pass…

Rubbish

Rubbish rubbish everywhere
And it was the gypsies fault
The dirty middens left their mark
They fled in the night when it was dark

Bags of filth open to see
The contents strewn bare
From tattie skins to dirty nappies
For people to stop and stare

And then the council have to come
And clean up after them
Their mark is gone and so is their pong
Of the gypsies and their rubbish

The Music Festival

Kagools, capes and wellies
Can be such a pain
Getting soaked but merry
In the pouring rain

Tents up and anchored in
Dotted here and there
Different shapes and sizes
With space and pods to share

Bands playing music
I hear a song or two
Listening very closely
I'm sure that is the "View"

Walking through the venue
I hear it loud and clear
The lovely music playing
I hear from ear to ear

Burger vans and hotdogs
Bacon butties and such
You can get your chips and coke
It doesn't cost that much

So summing it up
The music and all
I will be back
To this music festival

The Bad Taste Party

I go to a bad taste party
In the summer every year
I drink cider
My friend Sarah drinks beer

We all go by taxi
To Mel and Stan's
With our party clothes on
Making a stand

Some folk are dressed funny
Some folk are dressed scary
But the funniest of all
was a man called "Mary"

Dressed as black beauty
Wearing empty packets of meat
Adorned with spotted wellies
Upon extremely large feet

Well, the weather it rained
Then the sunshine came out
The band played a song
And we danced to "Twist and Shout"

We quenched our thirst
We were dehydrated
But before not too long
We were all inebriated

Partying on
In the summer night
Eating nibbles
And "Turkish delight"

Having laugh
And telling jokes
Drinking feeling merry
Aside funny dressed folk

It ended in the morning
It was way after dark
I went home to bed merry
Or was it "pissed as a fart"

In the cupboard the next morning
Raking for some Alka-Seltzer
I found a resolve
And was feeling much better

For reminiscing
Of the night gone past
I love the "Bad Taste Party"
Let's hope it's not the last!

The Car Boot Sale

Going to the car boot sale
In the sun or a howling gale
In all weathers you'll bare whatever
To find a bargain you will endeavour

Everything imaginable from A-Z
Nothing there surprises me
You will if you're lucky find bargains galore
You'll find that one then you'll want more

Squashed and shoved
In the hustle and bustle
You want that bargain
And get in a tussle

Laden with bags
You think you've enough
You spotted something else
But someone's got it so that's just tough

Time to go home
And load up your boot
Bags upon bags
Containing your loot

Until the next time
When you'll be looking again

For what is it called
Oh yes! That word BARGAIN!

The Edinburgh Tattoo

Up early in the car
Off to Edinburgh, it wizzna far
To the tattoo was our main event
The "Fringe" was on, artists came and went

Up and down the Royal Mile
Abidy gan aboot we a smile
The hustle and bustle in the city
It was far too busy and this was a pity

Trying to find a place to eat
Was no easy task and we thought defeat
But then we came across an Italian place
I thought to myself, "This looks ace"

We had our meal
The food and service was great
Although there wasn't loads on the plate
We left quite happy cos we had been fed
Now off to the tattoo "Canna wait we all said"

We all got seated and in position
Waiting in anticipation
There was a thunderous roar
The show had commenced
The pipers came out and in tartan were dressed

The different countries
From all around the world, performed in all their glory
And so that was the end of the "Tattoo"
And the end of my wee story!

The School Reunion (May 2015)

We had a school reunion
At the end of May
For it was 30 years
Since school was out the way

Into the big big world
Full of ventures new
Full of anticipation on life
Which just grew and grew

So I met with my old chums
From Lossiemouth High School
From 1980–1984
We were the kids that ruled

Some faces I did recognise
Some I didn't have a clue
I met with an old neighbour
His name was Andrew Kew!

People had got really tall
Some just still were small
Some were fat and some were thin
It was a mixed bag of everything

We all had a great time
We all had a blast
Reminiscing of our lives
And all that was in the past

So we all decided
To do it again
This class hook-up
This reunion

So in 3 years' time when we are 50
Starting our twilight years
We can look forward to growing old
In the next 20 years…

A Sign

Do you come from another place
To come and say "hello"
Are you happy and at peace
For that we just don't know

Don't be afraid to think of us
And wonder how we are
Your always in our thoughts and hearts
Your never very far

Do you look upon us
And keep us safe at night
With your arms wrapped around us
So cosy and so tight

I wish I saw you
Remembered your face
Your voice and touch
I would gladly embrace

I miss you so much
And look for a sign
To know that you're in heaven
And you are just doing fine…

Ghosties and Ghoulies

Ghosts and ghouls
That go bump in the night
Ghosties and ghoulies
Dare to give you a fright!

What do these wandering spirits want?
Floating in the night
They are there one minute
And then they're out of sight

Do they come to give you comfort
To let you know they are still here
To be an angel watching over you
To keep you safe and near

And then on the other hand
When your stuff goes missing
Or when it's been moved
From that position

And then it will turn up
Just out of the blue
Who put it there
You don't have a clue

So between their visions, their smells,
their touch and mischief
We long to be with our loved ones
In heaven and on earth…
Ghosts!

Who are you that visits
In the middle of the night?
Who are you that visits
And gives me such a fright?

A ghostly presence
An apparition
An old soul
Looking for recognition

A ghost that haunts you
From the past
Or is it a relative
That you have lost

They come in many
Shapes and forms
A face you knew or
Someone in a queue

Or is it a new-born
Who's come into the world?
Have they been here before?
Or am I being absurd
Then there are your pets
That barks into space
Is it a ghost that's
There in your face

Loved ones
That have been taken
You pray to see them
So they are never forsaken
To see them just for a moment
To recognise their smell their touch
Or to see their shadow
Can become all too much

So who are you?
And where are you now
You are in my mind my soul
Your visits now I think I can thole….

An angel who keeps me safe
Who sits on my shoulder
Who will be there when I am gone?
God grant me that it's not too long…

Memories

Memories of you
I have in my heart
Forever and a day
We were never apart

The angels came
And wrapped you in their wings
Carrying you off
To better things

A place in my heart
There will always be
Because Gran you meant
The world to me

Your memory, Gran
Will always live on
Like the sound of music
And words to a song

Forever and ever
I hope and I pray
That we are together
Again someday.

My Angels

I hope you are all happy,
Being good and full of glee
Remember Mammy misses you
And that's not easy for me

Mammy loves you both dearly
And hope it won't be long
Before I'm home and better
To my family where I belong

I miss your smiley faces
Your kisses and cuddles too
But in this poem my angels
I send my love to you

I hope you will forgive me for not being there for you
So hang in there don't worry and smile
Cos Mammy will be home for good
But it will take a little while

Reflection

Looking at me
And what do I see?
A body of lumps
Staring back at me

No curvy figure do I have
And jealous of some others
With their hourglass figures
They don't have to hide under the covers

I look at their bodies
Their lovely shape
Tall and slim
That make men gape

For I cannot stand
In a slender physique
For as fat as I am
I have my sorrows to seek

For my weight gives me pain
And slows me down
I'm like a humongous hippo
With a horrible frown

I'm jealous of these women
Their bodies so sleek
I want to have
That gorgeous physique

But instead I must suffer
And put up with that
All because
I am big and fat!

The Hysterectomy

You'll need a hysterectomy
The gynae stood and said
That'll solve the problem
As all I done was bled...

Three days later after my op
"You can go home now"
There's no more to chop

A wombless wonder
I thought to myself
And all this was done
For the good of my health

But too young to accept it
I'm not old enough for that
Oh just attend a meeting
For a coffee and a chat

As the years passed on
I felt robbed and cheated
For having the choice
Of my family completed

In coming to terms
And trying to believe
That I would never
Again conceive
So with my children now
The troubles and the glee
I sometimes think that it was right
This hysterectomy

We Miss You

Mam we miss you
We miss you my dear
Just to hold your hand
And keep you near

We miss you not phoning
Your deep husky voice
You were taken from us suddenly
You didn't have a choice

We miss not seeing you
To give you things that you liked
Jelly babies, Frye's cream
Pot noodles and the like

The grandkids miss your words of advice
Followed by your cheeky grin
They hold onto your memory
And keep it close within

I miss writing your letters
And telling you my views
Keeping you up to date
With all my "Dundee news"

I miss playing you at Scrabble
And you making up your words
Trying to get the magic seven
Some of them were absurd

We miss saying "I love you"
And giving you a bosey
After which you would smile
Because we made you cosy

So to our mam our granny
We just had to say
Until we meet again, angel
We'll keep the tears away!

The 50th Year School Reunion

I went to my school reunion
In September of this year
As all of us old classmates
Were in their 50th year

Before I went
My pal Gail and me
Got in the spirit
And had a wee "drinky"

We got all dolled up
And dressed smart casual
The night had begun
We were ready to have fun
But some of the friends I didn't know
I couldn't believe my eyes
And so the party had begun
We were in for a surprise

The surprise was them we did know
They looked so well and healthy
Some of them by gum
Were lucky in that they were wealthy

I listened to their stories
Of their life and how it had turned out
My life had been full of struggles
Compared to theirs, there was no doubt!
Some were in a business that had grew
Some were in business
making a good bob or two
I met an old friend his name was Andrew Kew

Some were designers
Another a teacher
One was a fisherman
The other a preacher

The night was buzzing
We were dancing and having fun
Then towards the end
The raffle had begun

We stood with our tickets
Waiting all excited
There were so many prizes
Going past our eyes

Last but not least
My number got shouted
I had wan the star prize
I couldn't believe my eyes

It was a Cashmere blanket
It was worth a lot of money
It was made in Johnston's Woollen Mill
Of Elgin up in Moray

Well, the night had been magic
It was drawing to a close
And for many a photo
I stood and struck a pose

Memories of what had been
Were now firmly implanted
And meeting up again
We were taking for granted

But we made a toast to absent friends
There was a couple who never made it
And their souls were taking early
To the gates that are so pearly

The night was a blast
My feet were aching
And so for a taxi home
We kept on waiting

Home we were and were reminiscing
Of the reunion that had just been
Of friendships rekindled and talking about the past
We had made new memories that were sure to last....

The Final Word

My funeral has come
Thy day to be done
On earth as it is in Heaven
Of my life to be told
Be it all far to bold

In part may I please be forgiven?
You'll sing my songs I love to hear
And recite some famous story
For thine is in Heaven not on earth
The power and the glory....

My time has come
And I'm carried to my final resting place
I see the look of sadness
Upon your tearful face...

As I'm laid down
And now I sleep
But my soul does not
And so it creeps!

Looking at the dirt
Being placed upon me
Shovel by shovel
Till I could no longer see
The flowers lay on top
For decoration
Of my life
And its celebration

And so as spirit I must now visit
Loved ones and my friends
For life as spirit in heaven all be it
Goes on and never ends….

My Dogs

My dogs keep me going
They keep my soul alive
I used to have four
But now I have five

All with their characters
Each with their needs
They run in a pack
It's like a stampede

I'll start with Harvey
King Farouk
In charge of his ladies
He's always on the look

Bella is funny
As she licks the floor
I often wonder
If her tongue is never sore

Lilly is boss
She speaks for the pack
She gets your attention
She's got some knack

Sadie is next
She jumps and wiggles
The oddball of the pack
She does make me giggle

Hattie is last
Always up to no good
Chewing what she can
And me if she could

They all play chases
Running back and fore
With boundless energy
As they run out the door

They love to lounge
About the couch
Each on a cushion
They slumber and slouch

They all love their deals
They all love a cuddle
They cosy all in
In one big huddle

So these are my dogs
Each to their own
They fill up my heart
And they fill up my home…

Downtown

I went downtown
In ma dressing gown
Hands in my head
Wearing a frown

I see a lavender bush
And I had a sigh
It had a whiff
As I walked on by

The sun came out
My mood was uplifted
I heard someone sing
They were truly gifted

I see in the distance
An oilrig sitting
I walked passed a garden
Someone was knitting

The woman looked elegant
She was wearing a scarf
With a porcupine on it
It made me laugh

I went to Kobie restaurant
And had a grapefruit juice

Then from the menu
I ordered octopus

Looking Back

I was thinking as I sat
Of my days diving
When the loch was like treacle
I looked down and saw a beetle

I ate my lunch
And thought of my day
Of all the things I had seen
That had come my way

I had ate octopus
Drinking grapefruit juice
Thought of me diving in treacle
And seeing that beetle

Seen the oilrig
Walked on by
And in doing this
I began to sigh

I passed the elegant lady
Wearing a scarf with porcupine
Took another look
And wished it was mine

Walked past the bush
Of lavender and
Had another sniff
Thinking to myself what a whiff

Got back home
And reflected on my day
Of everything that
Had come my way!

Heartache

Heartache comes
In different forms
From the one's you love
To the ones you have born

Disappointed…
In what they have done
My kids have let me down
Well, all bar one!

Thinking of where
And what went wrong
Cos a place in my heart
Is where they belong

But circumstances, choices
All come into play
I stand back and feel
Nothing but dismay

Advice I have given
Till I'm blue in the face
Wrong choices, wrong paths
All I feel is a disgrace!

So I'll carry on for
One day they will see

And the errors of their ways
Hopefully they will see!

My Window

Looking out my window
And what do I see?
The faces of people
Staring back at me

Some with their dogs
And some with their children
As I look across
At another building

My friends and neighbours
Live across the road
We often go there
To their humble abode

The school children pass
At a quarter to nine
Dawdling and some rushing
To get to school on time

The street cleaner passes
On a Thursday morning
The bin men come on Tuesday
Blue bins get emptied once a fortnight
Their day to come is a Friday

Then there's my neighbour
Washing his Jag
He does this while
Smoking a fag!

Cars and motorbikes
That zoom so fast with no consideration
They carry on like "Sterling Moss"
Driving recklessly at what cost?

So these are all the things I see
That pass time and pleases me
As I look out my wooden blinds
Depending on my state of mind...

"1/2 Past 2"

Half past two
and I canna sleep!
Half past two
and the birds go "cheep"!

I watch the clock
the hours dragging by
but there is no sleep
in this wink of an eye

For not a wink
of sleep I have had
and being up this early
Well, it's totally crud!

I decide to get up
and pass the time
I turn the radio on
while I sit and rhyme

It passes a while
and tires out my brain
I suffer from insomnia
but I try not to complain…

The sleepless nights
there is nothing worse
and so my dear friends
is the end of my verse!

Self-Portrait from a Broken Mirror

I look at all the pieces
The cracks not the creases
And think to myself what do I see
That each piece represents me…

A piece of whom I am inside
Troubled and somewhat sad
A piece to show me in thought
Of all my life that's been bad

But then there's the piece
Of another side sometimes bubbly and happy
A piece of me says hold your head high
To believe in myself and do not cry

Be happy with life
And the cards that I have been dealt
And do not judge people
Who are blessed with more wealth

Looking at the pieces
And me as a whole
Sensitive and caring
Trying to reach my goals

The mirror never lies
You see how you are
Embrace life it's a gift
It's a journey that goes far…

Each journey tells a story of emotions
We have endured; love yourself, for who you are,
Accept the things you cannot change and change the things you can
Yesterday has passed, live life for the day and tomorrow is never promised
I say this come what may

Winning the Lottery

Winning the lottery
What would I do?
Would I spend it on me?
Would I spend it on you?

Would I buy a house
Or would I buy a boat
People may think
That I'm trying to gloat

Would I stay in this country
Or would I stay home?
I might move to Marrakesh
I may go to Rome!

My family I would take care of
And pay off any debts
So they wouldn't have a worry
About bills or the mortgage or money

Butterflies

We went to St Andrews
To see the butterflies
And what we saw
We couldn't believe our eyes

The colours were magnificent
Bright and outstanding
But we had to be careful
Of where they were landing

Their house was hot
There was no air
I was sweating
And beginning to despair!

Some photographs I took
As I was having a look
At the butterflies in all their splendour
Oh how I loved this part of our adventure

We then went on to walk around the gardens
Admiring all the flowers
Around and down beside a stream
Seeing flowers we had never seen

Then went on for lunch
And walked up past the beach
And onto Grey Friars pub
For a drink and some grub

Going back to the bus
Feeling tired but uplifted
For what we had seen
Nature is truly gifted

If I Were Rich

If I were rich
What would I buy?
An aeroplane perhaps
To fly high in the sky

I would buy a house
Fit for a queen
The kind of house
Like you've never seen

I would buy
The homeless man a home
So he is warm
And not alone

I would look after animals
That was poorly treated
So they were not at the point
Of their lives being deleted

I would make sure
The NHS had plenty of staff
I would save the elephants
As well as the giraffes

I would buy research
Into finding a cure
For cancers and diseases
So our bodies were pure
I would buy a new body
And happy I'd be
If dreaming about money
Is nae the death of me!

Now You Are Gone

Every time I see you
you've grown a little more
Like the ache in my heart
Just grows a little more

I miss the not knowing
And having you near
Your touch and your voice
It's all gone my dear

My son you are
But a stranger you are now
You are distant and cold
In need of someone to hold

You look at me as if to say
What's she thinking about now?
I am your mother remember
Not some awkward bad cow!

I don't know what you are doing
From this day to the next
My emotions get out of control
And I am totally vexed

Diana

Diana
There will be no other
Who could give so much
In showing us love devotion and such

A princess you were
But a queen you will be
In the hearts of others
And that includes me

You made such a difference
You were a beacon of light
You were aware of life's problems
You tried to make them right

You are at peace now
As we all pray
May you know Diana
That in our hearts you will stay.

Grant

He's been working in Dundonald
For the past 4 years
And now he's leaving us
So let's shed a tear

He will be sadly missed
As will his quirky jokes
He likes to keep fit
And he doesn't smoke

He's into fitness in a big way
As he cycles in Lycra
from Carnoustie
Everyday

He has two lurcher dogs
His friends and his companions
He likes to take them for a run
Beating his times just for fun

The women think he's sexy
As he looks like "Kirk"
From Coronation Street
With a handsome smile
He's always neatly dressed
He's always smart
Hair never messed

He enjoys his TA weekends away
And he loves the endurance test
Seeing it as his challenge
Always giving it his best

He drives a Toyota Celica
In seductive dreamy black
Thinking he's a boy racer
He's the leader of the pack

So that's our Grant
Away to leave, away to pastures new
He will be missed by many
To name but a few

Jaimie Lee

An angel sent from heaven
A star that burns bright
She is my inspiration
My beacon that burns bright

She always has a smile
No matter how she's feeling
Her beautiful face with bonny blue eyes
To many is quite appealing

She works at Dundee Carers' Centre
Covering all aspects of work
Listening to others, solving problems
She is quite the bright spark

She is engaged to Barry
The love of her life
They plan to marry
And become man and wife

My beautiful daughter, loving kind
Always there for her dad and me
I wouldn't change anything about her
My gorgeous and caring Jaimie Lee…

Jamie

So many things left unsaid
So much shit
Going on in my head….

You left so sudden
When you went away
You broke my heart
On that fateful day

My brother I loved you
You know not how much
There will be no one to fill your shoes
No one as such

A special person
Qualities of a kind
You liked your "drammie"
I'll bear that in mind

Remember the times when we were little
Always being stupid and fickle
Up to no good the two of us would be
But best of buddies that was you and me

So you've away and left me
Your time had come
No more on this earth
To be done
I rage inside
Screaming and shouting
Asking myself

And always doubting
I can't find the answer
I feel I can't cope
All I can do
Is live in hope

I miss you my friend
I'll miss you for life
The emptiness I feel
Is even more rife

Help me through this
With an inner strength
Let me know you are there
I know you care

I hope you are happy
Besides Robbie, Mam and Dad
Knowing that then
it wouldn't be so sad

Give comfort to one another and watch over us
Looking at your photos, thinking you are not far away
I hope we will meet up in heaven
All together one day

Liz

No more "Speak up Brown yer through"
No more "Paddy fars your moo?"

She was the life and soul of the party
Whose life ended so shortly
Full of fun and laughter
A character to be sought after

She was larger than life
With her cinnamon hair
And would say what she thought
She just didn't care

A raw deal in life
Was the hand she was dealt
Why? I ask myself why?
I know why I know how but why her?

I have my happy memories
Of the wonderful person she was
Who was beaten by life and the cancer
You see that was the reason that was the cause

In memory of my dear friend
Liz Stewart
Who died 16 April 1999
Aged 38

Maisie

Big brown eyes that almost spoke
And a wet runny nose that would give you a poke
A big cheezie grin as she lay on the floor
And as for "pieces", she was always looking for more

She could open her crisps all on her own
And give you a paw when you were all alone
A faithful companion who would never let you down
Who would wag her tail even when I did frown

She would look into my face
And never say a word
She knew how I was feeling
Now ain't that absurd

I miss my friend I miss her so much
Her nose, her nudges, paws and waggly tail and such
But I'll remember her fondly forever in my heart
As memories of those we love they never go or part

Mandy

My CPN is called Mandy
She visits twice a week
She smiles and listens attentively
As all I do is speak

We try and have a laugh
Over coffee and a chat
And try to stay positive
About this and that

She's a wonderful woman
Young, free and single
Nothing at all
Like your average "Dingal"

She is caring and professional
And dresses extremely well
Will there be a man in her life
I hope so you just can't tell

Someone to share her laughter
Her sense of humour and fun
For Mandy is such a character
Of her kind there is only one

To share in her hopes and dreams
She waits for Mr Right

But Mandy, you know already
That your future is really bright....

My Dia

So gentle and kind
With a thrawn determination
"I've twa good sturdy legs"
This was his proclamation

Bonnet on out for a walk
In all kinds of weather
For a breath of fresh air
And a friendly old blether

Mowing his grass
Swiping up his leaves
Feeding the birdies
And cutting his trees

Pruning his roses
And clipping his hedge
"A bitty at a time"
That was his pledge

Never giving up
And never complaining
Getting on with life
That wasn't all "plain sailing"

He enjoyed watching the golf
And looking at the snooker
And tended to the stuff
That was boiling on the cooker

He enjoyed Robbie Burns
And would recite his works
He went to his friends' funerals
In all the different kirks

He used to enjoy a game of crib
His teeth fae of rum and occasional smoke
He was full of interesting stories
And could still crack a joke

"Accept the things you cannot change"
He always used to say
Intelligent and wise he was
In whatever came his way

Devoted to Jessie
His wonderful wife
Who meant everything to him
This was his life

My Pal Gail

For over 30 years
Through ups and downs
Good times and bad
When I am happy
And when I am sad!

Nothing is a bother
She takes it in her stride
A worry or a confidence
That I have inside

She can talk forever
In an upbeat way
She makes me laugh
Oh she makes my day!

She'll try and advise me
And put things right
I know I can call her
Day or night

We have so much in common
We know how we tick
We know and feel
What gets on each another's wicks

I love her to bits
I will luv her to the end
She is very special
She is my best friend....

My Son

The fight is over
But it's only begun
To make them suffer
After what they have done

For not listening for years
And not taking you true
For making you wait
After all that we had been through

But help is at hand now
So reach out and grab it
Hold your head high
And rise above it

It will ease your pain
And your frustration
And help you with
Your concentration

To help you understand life
The rotten cards you were dealt
My heart can only go out to you
Always remember that Mammy loves you

Niave

You have been here for 3 ½ years
And are moving on to chapters new
You'll be missed by many
It won't be just a few

You live in Fordoun
It's near Laurencekirk
You'll have to commute to Aberdeen
But you'll be central for work

Your partner Daryl upcycles furniture
Giving it a new lease of life
And who knows one day
You could become his wife!

Your family live in Ireland
They live in Kilcool
You miss them dearly
It is a big pull

You love to cook
Great dishes you make
It doesn't stop there
You do a grand home bake

You don't brush your hair
So people despair
When brushed it's beautiful
Bonny and fair

Playing your shinty
Camen in hand
With a skilful eye
You are the best in the land!

You are also in the brownies
With all the little mites
Helping them earn their badges
And preventing any fights!

You love your running, Zumba
And fitness classes
Doing the kettle bells and boxercise
Where you have to watch your glasses

So we all say goodbye
And wish you all the best
You'll be sorely missed
By myself and the rest…

You Are Gone

Every time I see you
You've grown a little more
Like the ache in my heart
Grows until it's sore

I miss the not knowing
And having you near
Your touch and your voice
It's all gone my dear

My son you are
But a stranger you are now
You are distant and cold
In need of someone to hold

You look at me as if to say
What she thinking about now
I am your mother remember
Not some awkward bad cow!

I don't know what you are doing
From this day to the next
My emotions get out of control
And I am totally vexed....

On This, Your Wedding Day

On 31st of August
At 2:30 pm
In the Queens Hotel
Nethergate
Dundee.

Damien and Jenny
You are now man and wife
Treasure each other
For the rest of your life

Memories are precious
Words are too
Love one another from the moment
That you both said "I Do"

Congratulations to you both
Luv from
Gran and Granda
xxx

On Your Retirement

On your retirement we would like to remind you
In case your memory packs in
That you are a grandpa and married to Linda
And smoke the pipe for your sins

You have a head of silver hair
And hardly a wrinkle in sight
You're never lost for words you see
And with the doors you'll fight

You hold out your hand
For your pocket money
From your Linda
Your one true honey

Up to here with women
And especially Mandy's phone
You hate its constant ringing
Coz you canna work your own

You have a musical talent
Playing the guitar in a band
You were a painter and decorator
With a brush in your hand

On Your Retirement

Here is a list for you to remember
On becoming an OAP on the 14th of November

Some falsers you have
But can expect some more
To complement your hairy ears
And wrinkles galore
With creaking joints
And the fading vision
And the constant running back and fore
For continual pushing

With more loss of hair
And the thinning of skin
Along with memory loss
Where you can't mind a thing

So look forward to this
In your retirement
And try not to be
Overwhelmed by it!

Black Days

Black days my mind a haze
What am I to do?
Despair and no laughter
Is how it feels for ever after?

The pain I'm in
Is a terrible sin
The torment is torture
I cannot win

For the feeling of nothing
Of numbness as if dead
With all of the shit
That goes on in my head!

Oh help me God
For guidance and salvation
For I feel as if I have death
By invitation

For it beckons me
To come and see
If it will be the
Death of me!

So with some help
Starts the healing
And death to me
Is no longer appealing

For I can see that
We all have a choice
As we listen inside
To the infamous voice!

Worries

Another poem
Of what's gone on
My list of worries
Goes on and on

Thinking of the past
And all that has happened
Leaves me nothing less
Than saddened

So to "New Year" I say this
Be good to me
This year
And don't take the piss

Don't lade me with worry
Upset and strife
I want to be able
To love my life

To be at peace with
One and all
I leave it up to you
It is your call

www.ingramcontent.com/pod-product-compliance
Lightning Source LLC
LaVergne TN
LVHW011210250125
802092LV00007B/208